BOLD KIDS

A CHILDREN'S BOOK INTERESTING AND INFORMATIVE FACTS

No part of this book may be reproduced or used in any way or form or by any means whether electronic or mechanical, this means that you cannot record or photocopy any material ideas or tips that are provided in this book.
Copyright 2022

All images in this book have been reproduced with the knowledge and prior consent of the artists concerned, and no responsibility is accepted by producer, publisher, or printer for any infringement of copyright or otherwise, arising from the contents of this publication.

When you are looking for some cool facts about Wisconsin for kids, you should start by reading up on its famous cheese! Although Wisconsin is known as America's Dairyland, the state is not only known for its famous cheese, but for a lot of other cool things as well!

Before the Civil War, people from Wisconsin met to discuss stopping the spread of slavery. The meeting resulted in the founding of the Republican Party. The Democratic Party has its roots in the State of Massachusetts.

In 1844, the state was an important part of the Underground Railroad, which helped escaped slaves reach Canada. The Underground Railroad was named after Wisconsin because of the many people who managed to escape slavery. In fact, over one million people were freed from slaves in the state.

Another fun fact about Wisconsin for kids is that it is home to the oldest mammoth bones in the world, which are 14,500 years old. These bones were found in the state of Michigan. The hunters of mammoths settled in Wisconsin thousands of years ago.

The state's history has been filled with fascinating stories about the first peoples of the country. They are the Winnebago, Menominee, Ojibwe, and Pottawatomi, and they live in the state today.

For children, Wisconsin has many things to explore. The state is home to over one million dairy cows, producing more cheese than anywhere else in the United States. The land has beautiful rolling hills that provide ideal grazing grounds for bovine. Scientists discovered that human life in Wisconsin began more than 14,000 years ago.

The state is also a leading producer of cranberries, which grow in bogs that were left behind when ice age glaciers melted. The state is heavily forested, and timber is harvested in the northern part of the state and used to make paper and other products.

The state's names are derived from its two major rivers, the Mississippi and the Wisconsin. The state is a relatively flat region, with two major rivers and many lakes. Its borders are with Minnesota and Michigan.

There are several interesting facts about Wisconsin for kids, which will keep your children entertained for hours. The state is home to two state capitals and four major cities. The largest city is Milwaukee. With its population of 5.8 million people, the Badger is one of the largest in the country.

The state has many fun symbols. Its state flowers are the wood violet and its state insect is the Western honey bee. The state tree is the sugar maple. The state fish is the muskellunge.

The cow is the state animal. Its most famous river is the Mississippi. The largest river in Wisconsin is the Mississippi. The Badger's name is based on the French "Wisconsin."

In the 18th century, the first Europeans reached the area. It was under British rule in 1763, but this didn't change the country's geography. Later on, settlers fought against the Native Americans, but ultimately, the French helped the state become a state.

The city of Milwaukee is the state's largest, and is the largest city. The U.S. federal government's headquarters are in Madison.

The state's motto is "Forward". Its state flower is the wood violet. Its state insect is the Western honey bee. The state tree is the sugar maple. The state animal is the muskellunge.

The Badger's motto is "Forward" and its residents are known as Wisconsinites. The state's largest city is Milwaukee. This is the most populous state in the nation.

The state's motto is "Forward." In addition, the state is also home to the Western honey bee, the state flower is the wood violet, and the state fish is the muskellunge. It is the only state to have two river states.

The capitol of Wisconsin is Madison. The motto means "Forward." The Republican party is the main political party of the United States. While Wisconsin is located in the Midwest, it is bordered by Illinois and Minnesota.